THE
Archive Photographs
SERIES
ST IVES BAY

THE
Archive Photographs
SERIES

ST IVES BAY

Compiled by
Jonathan Holmes

CHALFORD

First published 1995
Copyright © Jonathan Holmes, 1995

The Chalford Publishing Company
St Mary's Mill, Chalford,
Stroud, Gloucestershire, GL6 8NX

ISBN 0 7524 0186 6

Typesetting and origination by
The Chalford Publishing Company
Printed in Great Britain by
Redwood Books, Trowbridge

Dedication

To my nephews, Joseph and Saul Stevens

Contents

Introduction

The sweeping form of St Ives Bay with its rugged cliffs and sandy beaches makes it one of the most picturesque parts of Great Britain. This volume is intended to show that the Bay has many different facets from the quaint old fishing town of St Ives to the once important industrial town of Hayle. The chapters have been organised to give the reader an anti-clockwise view of the Bay, starting in St Ives, moving around the coast through Hayle, and eventually coming to Gwithian and Godrevy.

St Ives was first and foremost a fishing port and during the last century many millions of pilchards were caught and sent from here to London and the Bay of Naples in Italy. The fishing tradition still continues but today the tourist trade takes pre-eminence over everything else. Many of the cottages around the harbour are now holiday homes and flats and no longer does the smell of fish pervade the harbour area and these little cottages. The arrival of the railway to St Ives brought the tourists and with them came the need for grand hotels, probably the most famous of which is the Tregenna Castle Hotel but equally important is the Porthminster Hotel.

Along with the tourists came the artists which later made St Ives internationally famous as an artists' colony. The artist Turner visited St Ives in 1811 but it was not until seventy years later when artists such as Julius Olson, Louis Grier and Anders Zorn came to St Ives and stayed, that St Ives became known for its artists.

In 1928 Christopher Wood and Ben Nicholson visited St Ives and came across the work of the naive artist Alfred Wallis and this can be seen as the beginning of what today is known as the St Ives Modernist Period. Later Dame Barbara Hepworth, Peter Lanyon and Ben Nicholson settled in the town and brought the colony international fame. The formal recognition of this eventually came with the opening of the new Tate Gallery in St Ives in 1993 under the curatorship of Michael Tooby.

St Ives would not normally be thought of as a town where textiles were manufactured but they were, under the name of Crysede. Crysede had shops throughout Britain and mail order customers world-wide.

Carbis Bay and Lelant where also important in the growth of the tourist industry with beaches of shimmering golden sands. Hayle has for many years advertised itself as 'Three Miles of Golden Sands' buts its industrial heritage is more important. Once Hayle was a hive of activity and some of the largest steam engines the world has ever seen were built in the foundry of Harvey's and Sons. In the late 1770s John Harvey, a blacksmith, from Gwinear moved his forge to Carnsew on the Hayle estuary. There he established an iron foundry, the first in Cornwall, complete with a reverberatory furnace, sheds, workshops and a boring mill. Harvey had recognised that there was a critical need for iron pipes, pumps and engine parts for the expanding mine industry. The firm later went on to build ships. The foundry was sold for scrap in 1908/9 but the company continued to trade after this as a builders' merchants, eventually being taken over by U.B.M. It now trades under the Jewsons banner. Another foundry existed at Copperhouse and the town boasted two smelting works. Today Hayle resembles a ghost town with much of its industrial heritage demolished or not recognised. At the turn of the century the town also had a large dynamite works on the Towans with nearly 2,000 people working there during the First World War.

Probably the most obvious feature of the Bay is the lighthouse at Godrevy whose job is to warn vessels of the treacherous reef. A buoy marks the reef itself.

Jonathan Holmes
Museum Officer
Penzance and District Museum and Art Gallery

One
St Ives: The Town

Porthminster c. 1875. The railway had yet to be built and the seine boats drawn up on the beach pre-date the town's importance as a tourist resort.

Tregenna Hill looking from Trenwyn Gardens around the turn of the last century. Top left can be seen the coastguard houses and the lookout.

The Board School at the Stennack under construction in 1880. Behind is Wheal Ayr and to the left Eden House the home of the Treweekes.

An interior view of the Board School. The blackboard states that the date is the 23rd January 1902. The stern looking schoolmaster is Mr Kaye.

The fishing fleet outside St Ives harbour c. 1904. In the foreground cattle are being fed in the grounds of the Tregenna Castle Hotel.

Tregenna Castle Hotel, St Ives. Construction of the building was started in 1774 and the architect was John Wood. The castellated detail was added around 1844 along with a further ten rooms. In 1878 it was leased to the Great Western Railway and opened as a hotel. In 1895 the railway company purchased the freehold of the property.

Porthminster Hotel 1910. The hotel opened in 1894 and has recently celebrated its centenary. In the foreground can be seen the seine boats and to the right is the signal box for the railway station.

The Terrace with the Porthminster Hotel in the foreground in about 1895.

Porthminster Beach c. 1910. Down by the sea can be seen bathing machines while further up, above the high watermark, are a number of seine boats. At middle right can be seen the engine-shed where the locomotive used on the St Ives branch-line was stabled overnight.

Porthminster Beach c. 1904. No bikinis here, you were expected to be fully clothed at all times in those days. It was not until the 1930's that it was thought acceptable for ladies and gentlemen to be seen partially dressed in public! The fashion of the period demanded that many layers of clothing be worn and it is surprising that the ladies did not swoon with the affects of the sun and heat.

Porthminster Beach c. 1936. The beach cafes had been built to cater for the needs of the sun-worshippers, while bathing machines had been superseded by tents. Many a happy Sunday School Tea Treat has been staged on these golden sands.

This card was posted in St Ives on the 17th August 1917. 'Had lovely weather since we have been down here ..., Love Jessie'.

Pednolver Rocks on the edge of Porthminster Beach c. 1915.

Porthminster Beach, 1930. Flags can be seen flying from the Malakoff while a flotilla of boats are just visible off Pednolver Point.

Porthmeor Beach and the Island, 1900. No sign of surfers or bathers here! The little girl is wearing a straw hat, extremely popular headgear during the late Victorian and Edwardian years.

Entrance to Thicket, St. Ives   My time has been very pleasantly filled in here

A saucy postcard from about 1910.

St. Ives. Porthmeor Beach.

Porthmeor Beach c. 1910, complete with bathing machines and deck chairs. In the distance can be seen Clodgy Point.

54194. Treloyhan Manor, St. Ives.

Treloyan Manor built to the design of the well-known Cornish architect Silvanus Trevail in 1892. It was built for the Hain family and on the death of Lady Hain in 1927 it was sold. It later opened as a hotel in 1930. In 1947 it was acquired by the Wesley Guild, opening under their management in 1948.

St Ives railway station. The existence of the Broad Gauge track in the station dates this photograph to before 1892, as in that year the track was realigned to the Standard Gauge. In the background can be seen the wooden pier on which construction started in 1864. It is probable that this photograph dates from around 1880.

Porthminster Point c. 1904. A saddle tank locomotive is waiting to bring in the coaches, which can be seen on the viaduct, into the station. The engine shed can be clearly seen along with its all important watertank.

Day visitors alighting from a train c. 1925. The nine coach train could have been a 'special' coming from one of the other Cornish holiday resorts. This possibility seems to be confirmed by the fact that the passengers are not carrying any luggage.

Mrs Barber at 8, Pudding Bag Lane. She was the wife of Moll Barber who was famous for his carving of 'Joanies', wooden dolls carved from scraps of wood.

Moll Barber is seen here carving a boat, although he was more famous for his carved 'Joanies'. These dolls were often carved from old oars or driftwood.

Local building workers erecting properties on Carrick Dhu just off Windsor Hill c. 1910.

The Salvation Army spring cleaning England's Net Factory where they held services before the Citadel was built.

The Island Battery c. 1880. These Napoleonic guns were dismantled and removed in 1895. In the background can be seen the building we know today as St Nicholas's Chapel.

The Old House on the Island, c. 1880, otherwise known as St Nicholas's Chapel.

The Cliffe, Fore Street, c. 1890. On the left can be seen Comley's Outfitting and Boot and Shoe Warehouse. The lights state 'Very Lowest Prices', 'Boots Repaired', and 'Tennis Shoes'.

T.T. Trevorrow's butchers shop c. 1930. In the window can be seen turkeys, beef, lamb and butter.

View from the Market Place to Wills Lane c. 1890.

High Street c. 1914. On the left is the Consolidated Bank of Cornwall while on the right a grocer advertises all kind of merchandise from 'Melox' dog food to 'Anglo Ales'.

William John Cooper in the doorway of his shop at 3, Fore Street, c. 1905. He operated a photographic business from the same premises.

Mr J. Richards posing outside his bakery shop in Gabriel Street in about 1910 with his wife, staff and two delivery carts.

Mr A. Ward, who ran a bakery near the harbour, is seen here on his delivery round at Higher Stennack, c. 1910.

A general store in St Ives c. 1900. The exact whereabouts of this shop is unknown. The shop advertises Cadbury's Cocoa and Nestles Milk. The windows are crammed with all sorts of foodstuffs.

WE SELL...
AND RECOMMEND

DUNLOP TYRES

AND ACCESSORIES

W. GUPPY & SONS,
Talland Garage,
St. Ives, CORNWALL.
Phone : 245.

L,L, 45

Many businesses gave out
postcards as a form of advertising.

Eastmans Limited c. 1910. On
the news board behind the
policeman can be read 'Visitor
Drowned at Penzance', 'Reform
Government Majority Commons'
and 'Vanishing Scene'.

J. M. Thomas and Son's grocery shop
c. 1920.

Tregenna Place c. 1910. On the right can be seen Williams Bazaar and on the left the turret of the Public Library. The foundation stone of the library was laid by the donor J. Passmore Edwards in 1896. The library opened on the 20th April 1897.

The George and Dragon public house situated in the Market Place offered a welcome drink on market day, c. 1880. It was demolished in 1887.

M. Stevens Tobacconist c. 1920. In the window can be seen advertisements for Gold Flake, Capstan Navy Cut, and Robin, some of which are still well-known names.

Market Place c. 1880. On the left is the Golden Lion Inn. Also in the square itself was the George and Dragon.

The hawker S. Barrett at the end of Fore Street, Chy-an-Chy, next to the Slipway, c. 1890. He came from Ludgvan to sell his wares to the holiday makers visiting St Ives.

Chy-an-Chy c. 1900 with the Primitive Chapel, built in 1837, behind. The chapel was made famous by the artist W.H.Y. Titcomb who depicted the interior of the chapel. His most famous painting, 'Primitive Methodists at Prayer', is in Dudley Art Gallery.

Harbour beach c. 1900. This was a favourite playground for the town's children and a place of bustle when the boats were landing their catches.

The Sloop Inn c. 1910. Probably the most famous public house in St Ives. It featured, along with Barnoon Cemetery, in the film *Raise the Titanic*.

Quay Row c. 1910. The beach was used for all sorts of activities from mending nets to hanging out the weekly wash.

Looking from the site of the present lifeboat-house towards the Sloop Inn. Large boats were often beached for unloading and repair. The Wharf Road had yet to be built.

Quay Row c. 1900. On the left is Quick's sail loft while outside Mr Stevens's shop the old men of the town put the world to rights.

Shaw's Popular Café, Fore Street, c. 1910. The tables were decorated with flowers and laid with linen serviettes and tablecloths, a far cry from the average café of today.

One of many streets of fishermens' cottages that can still be seen in St Ives. Many were three storey with a ground floor fish cellar where pilchards were prepared and pressed.

Posted on 24th February 1908, this quaint postcard view of a St Ives' court was published by Valentine. One of the women is holding a water pitcher. There was no running water in those days, you collected your water every day from the nearest well or waterspout.

Probably photographed on some sort of special occasion, as the people in the picture are dressed in their 'Sunday best', these houses show very clearly that the family lived in the first and second floors while the work was done on the ground floor.

The harbour beach with the catch laid out. This view probably dates from about 1925.

Carnglaze Street, looking towards the harbour. The postmark on this postcard is 17th April 1909.

Capel Court c. 1900. The walls of the cottages on the right have huge granite buttresses to keep them up and between them is an entrance to a fish cellar.

The Digey c. 1910. On the top step can be seen a trough used to do the weekly washing. The old fishwife is knitting. Each fishing port had their own distinctive design of fishermens' guernseys. It is said that if a body was lost at sea it was easy to tell from which port the man came.

The old granite cottages of the fishermen were small but cosy. The fish cellars underneath their homes meant that the smell of fish was always with them. Fish oil was used for cooking and lighting the cottages. A special type of oil lamp was used called a 'chill'.

Skidden Hill. This steep hill runs up to and finishes by the Catholic Church which opened in 1908.

Virgin Street c. 1905. This postcard was printed in Saxony in Germany. Before the First World War the majority of postcards were printed in Germany. Many holiday souvenirs were also made in Germany and sold in St Ives.

St Ives Parish Church was dedicated to St Ia. It is constructed from granite brought by sea from Zennor. It was built between 1411 and 1426.

St Ives War Memorial. The unveiling ceremony took place on 2nd November 1922.

St Ives church. This church owned the first organ to be installed in Cornwall but, along with the rood screen, this was removed by the Puritans in 1647. The spectacular barrel roofs plus the Mediaeval carvings make this one of the most beautiful churches in Cornwall.

The fishing nets were once all made by hand but by the middle of the nineteenth century machines were built to manufacture them. This machine was used at Mr England's works which was situated in North Place. This photograph dates from around 1920.

Green Tin Mine, Trink Hill. Situated two miles south west of St Ives it was part of St Ives Consols. It reopened in 1905 but closed again in 1923. This group of men have just used explosive to bring down the mines old winding gear.

St Ives Consols, Power House. The postcard is the work of S.J. Govier, a photographer from Chacewater.

Wheal Trenwith, a section of St Ives Consolidated Limited.

Crysede was founded by Alec Walker in 1919 when he bought a row of cottages in Newlyn. The company moved to St Ives in 1925 when Tom Heron was appointed as manager. Alec Walker's spectacular semi-abstract designs can be seen in the collections of Penzance Museum and Art Gallery and the Royal Cornwall Museum, Truro.

The Crysede factory on the Island. Originally a pilchard cellar and later a parachute factory, today it is the site of St Nicholas's Court.

Alec Walker inspecting a piece of Crysede silk c. 1925.

Keith Ross carving a printing block, watched by Tom Heron. Tom Heron's son is the well-known St Ives artist Patrick Heron. These blocks were used to print the designs onto the silk. Some designs used at least six different blocks to produce the required pattern.

Hand block printing at the Island Works, St Ives. Norman Gilbert is in the foreground. The silk was pinned to a calico wrapper. Seen alongside the printer is his assistant. These lads were known as 'wipers'.

A Jersey Car setting out from St Ives c. 1890. J.H. Tremayne of the Western Hotel is driving. These cars took visitors to local towns and beauty spots.

The Cornish Fire Brigade visiting the town in the 1930s. The exact date is unknown.

Men and machines were paraded down through the narrow streets.

Headed by St Ives first motorised fire engine the firemen marched along Fernlea Terrace behind the Town Band.

The Mayor of St Ives processing to Knill's Monument in about 1900. In front of him are two constables carrying their staffs of office.

John Knill was the Collector of Customs in St Ives from 1762 to 1782. He was then sent to Jamaica to re-organise their customs system. It is said that his scruples weakened and he became an owner of a privateer. Knill was to be interred in this monument, built in 1782, on his death, but this did not happen. His will directed that ten girls under fourteen and dressed in white, along with two widows and a fiddler were to walk in procession to the monument. They were to dance around the monument and then sing the Hundredth Psalm. For this the girls received ten shillings (50p) and the widows one pound. This custom is still carried out in each year that ends in a one or a six.

Two
St Ives: The 1894 Flood

The heavens opened on the night of the 14th November 1894, following a period of very wet weather that had left the ground already waterlogged. Dr J. Nicholls recorded a rain fall of three inches in under three hours! The torrent is seen here passing the Wesleyan Chapel.

Chapel Street, looking from the front of the Wesleyan Chapel towards the crowd in the previous picture.

Water pouring through the railings below the Tregenna Castle Hotel.

It was a scene of fascination and disbelief.

As the water receded the damage started to become all to obvious.

The force of the water had ripped up the road surface.

A great section of the road had disappeared!

Looking down Tregenna Hill with the flood water flowing down towards the harbour and the sea.

A view of further damage, probably recorded further up the Stennack.

The damage in Tregenna Place.

Three
St Ives: The Harbour, Fishing and Boat Building

St Ives Harbour c. 1900. Children in smocks beachcomb in a harbour that is full of boats.

Smeaton's Pier c. 1900. The pier was extended in 1890. The original lighthouse designed by Smeaton in 1831 can be seen half way down the pier.

Wharf Road has yet to be built and the houses back right onto the harbour itself. The slipway was used to launch the lifeboat.

This postcard view is entitled 'Old Houses, St Ives'. This view is looking from the pier towards the Wharf Road. On the beach can be seen a number of traditional fishing boats known as Luggers.

This is the *Emily SS27* chained up in the harbour while in the distance can be seen Porthminster Point. This postcard is postmarked 20th December 1904.

Landing the fish c. 1900. The cane baskets known as kitts were filled with fish and then loaded onto carts which took them to the harbour side or to a fish cellar.

Boys will be boys! The fascination that water holds for children is still just as great. In the background can be seen the fishing fleet airing and drying its sails.

St Ives from the pier c. 1900. In the background can be seen the Terrace, Porthminster Hotel and the Railway Station.

The Harbour is filled with boats c. 1900. The vessel in the foreground has the distinguished registration SS1. The legs on the sides of these boats were put on when they came into harbour so that they would remain upright whatever the state of the tide.

This view and the next pre-date the building of the Wharf Road. Both date from around 1900. It was not until 1922 that the Wharf Road was constructed.

The area was a place to contemplate, smoke your baccy, catch up with the gossip or just to do the daily job of gutting the catch.

Three of the local Gigs, c. 1900, *Daisy*, *Lander*, and *Mystery*. The man tipping his hat is George Tipping.

The Harbour. In the background can be seen either a vessel in for repair or under construction, while a forest of masts bear evidence to the large number of vessels in port.

A fishing lugger entering the harbour c. 1900.

Mending a seine net c. 1890. This view was probably taken on the Island.

The St Ives fishing fleet departing for the fishing grounds, with SS8 *Mary* in the foreground, c. 1900.

Leaving the harbour and home for the wild ocean. These men went out to sea in all weathers to provide for their families and the community.

The boat on the left is *LT236 Ethel* from Lowestoft and on the right is the local boat, *SS96 Manx Girl*.

The seine net has been cast and now it will be drawn in, hopefully catching the shoal of fish sighted by the huer. Seine fishing used one large net to encompass a whole shoal. The boat carrying the net was directed by a man on land who could see the shoal known as the huer. He used a furze, a branch dipped in white wash or covered in cloth, to direct the boat. In later years paddles were used that were not unlike large Ping Pong bats.

The net is now boiling with fish and in the background can be seen Porthminster Beach.

The net is full to overflowing. The weight of the fish in the boat that is being loaded is being counterbalanced by the weight of the bow of another boat.

Using baskets and nets, the main seine net is gradually emptied.

Preparing or cleaning the nets on Porthminster Beach.

Bringing the haul into the harbour and loading it onto the carts c. 1910.

Gutting and preparing the catch on the Wharf c. 1920.

Packing fish on the Wharf ready for their long journey by rail to London and beyond.

The whole community was employed in the fishing industry. This view of the Wharf dates from around 1920 and shows a scene of hustle and bustle.

The Fish Market c. 1900. The baskets are filled with fish which the women have just sorted.

Bulking pilchards and dry salting them in Maid Betsey's cellar in the year of the great pilchard season of 1871. The Barnaloft Flats were built on the site of this cellar.

WHEN THE BOATS COME IN. 10.3.21

Edwin Couch and his niece Bessie Bessiman, who was then aged five, photographed by Valentine. This photograph was a commercial success for the photographer and many thousands of postcards were produced of it.

The *Unity PZ286* being launched at Porthgwidden c. 1880.

The *Casabianca* was built on the harbour beach in 1877.

Four
Carbis Bay,
Lelant and St Erth

Carbis Valley, c. 1880, with the ruined engine house of East Providence on the right. This was the site of Annies Picnic Grounds, a popular place for Sunday School Tea Treats.

Hawkes Point Cottage, in 1884, was one of only three houses in Carbis Bay. Carbis Bay at that time was more commonly known as Carbis Valley.

Carbis Bay in 1920. In the foreground is the Carbis Bay Hotel. By this time many more houses had been built, some of them as guest houses for the growing tourist trade.

Looking towards Hawkes Point in about 1912. In the distance can be seen the residence of the Hain family, Treloyan Manor.

F_43113. ST. IVES: CARBIS BAY.

Carbis Bay 1920. The beach is filling up with bathers and changing tents can be seen on the sands.

A postcard dating from 1905 showing the bay and its viaduct with a train heading towards St Ives.

On the sands in 1910. In the background can be seen a type of bathing machine. Paddling seems to be the order of the day for the children.

Carbis Bay Station c. 1910 with a train ready to depart to St Erth Station. Connections could be caught to London and elsewhere in Britain. St Erth Station was at one time called St Ives Road.

Leaving Carbis Bay for St Ives, this 2-6-2 tank locomotive has a light load with just two coaches.

Abbey Hill, Lelant, c. 1900.

Lelant in about 1915. On the right can be seen the Lelant Hotel, now the Badger Inn.

This road in Lelant leads down towards the church and the dunes. This postcard was franked in 1910 and is marked as being a 'genuine Kodak card'.

Lelant Fair, a view that probably dates from around 1900. On the left can be seen Moncini and Volanti's ice cream wagon from Camborne. They are credited as being the people who introduced ice cream to Cornwall.

The Ferry, Lelant

Lelant Ferry, a service that operated from here as it was the shortest route to St Ives. Before the building of the Causeway it would have been necessary to go via St Erth and cross the river there.

Lelant Station, c. 1880, in broad gauge days, with a spur to Lelant Wharves on the right.

Lelant Station in 1939, this pretty little station was sold and is now a private house although the trains still stop on their way to St Ives.

Hayle from Lelant c. 1920. In the foreground is the ship breakers yard of Ward and Sons.

St Erth Parish Church c. 1910. The only form of illumination available was with oil lamps.

The old coach at Trewinnard. This coach can now be seen at the Royal Cornwall Museum, Truro.

Five
Hayle: The Town

Hayle harbour c. 1910. On the right is the shipyard of Harvey's of Hayle. In the foreground can be seen a traction engine used to pull the heavy loads to and from the harbour. These loads included wood, coal, machinery, tin and copper ore.

The St Ives fishing fleet leaving Hayle on the high tide c. 1890.

Hayle from the Towans, c. 1900, with the chimneys of the foundry visible in the background.

Hayle from Lelant Ferry in about 1910. In the distance can be seen St Elwyn's Church, while in the foreground the ferry boat is seen leaving to cross the estuary.

Two St Ives fishing boats making their way to sea with the Towans in the background c. 1890.

The Millpond, Hayle, c. 1900. This whole area has recently been refurbished by the Town Council.

The Plantation, Hayle, c. 1906.

Foundry Square, Hayle, c. 1900. On the left is the Market House which was partially destroyed by fire, the upper storey being demolished. The lower part was refurbished and is today the home of Lloyds Bank.

Highlanes, Hayle. This view from a postcard dates from c. 1900.

Highlanes Avenue, Hayle, c. 1900, looking up the hill towards Hayle Community School.

Penpol and Clifton Terraces c. 1900. The track was originally part of the Hayle railway which opened in 1837. It ran from Hayle to Redruth with branches to Tresavean and Portreath.

Penpol Terrace c. 1910. The shop, which is presently Bigglestons, has not changed at all. The horse-drawn vehicle in the foreground is waiting for its owner who has perhaps gone shopping.

Penpol Terrace, c. 1910, this time looking towards the foundry end of Hayle.

Shunting on the railway around the wharves at Hayle was accomplished by horses until their retirement in 1961 when they were replaced by tractors.

Hayle Terrace and St Elwyn's Church c. 1900.

Fore Street, Copperhouse, Hayle. On the right can be seen the Cornubia Hotel. In recent years the columns have unfortunately been replaced with concrete pillars.

Copper Terrace c. 1900. The wasteland in the foreground is now the site of Leo's supermarket.

Hayle Regatta, 13th August 1904. The regatta was a major event in Hayle's social calendar. It was originally established in 1837 through the efforts of Mr O'Neale who was the principal Customs Officer for Hayle.

Preparing for the race in 1904. St Elwyn's Church is visible in the background. Along the street can be seen various sideshows and stalls.

The Tub race, Hayle Regatta, 1904.

Phillack from the Copperhouse side of the pool.

Undercliff, Phillack, c. 1910.

Phillack Church c. 1904.

The parish stocks at Phillack, Hayle, c. 1900. This rare photograph by Gibson and Sons, Penzance, is especially interesting because these very stocks have recently been rediscovered in a building near the church.

Hayle Towans, c. 1906. On the cliff top can be seen the building which was to become Taylor's Tea Rooms.

Taylor's Tea Rooms, c. 1910, where many a Sunday School Tea Treat was held.

Guildford Viaduct, Hayle. This shows construction of the present granite viaduct while the original wooden viaduct designed by Brunel was still in use. This recently discovered photograph dates from 1885/1886. The new viaduct came into service on the 5th October 1886.

Six
Hayle: Industries

ELECTRIC WORKS.

Hayle Power Station viewed from across the estuary. The power station opened in 1909 and was the main source of power for Cornwall. Coal was brought by sea and by rail. As well as domestic supply it also powered the Camborne and Redruth Tramway.

Hayle from the air, July 1956. This photograph was taken for the Associated Ethyl Co Limited. The many remnants of Hayle's once glorious industrial past can be seen scattered all over the town.

The Associated Ethyl Works outfall in 1953. The Steam Packet Inn and the cottages in the central band of the picture have been demolished and the town's swimming pool now stands on the site of this outfall.

The Associated Ethyl Works 12th May 1955. The plant extracted bromide from sea water, starting operations in 1940.

A six ton steam hammer in the forge at Harvey's Foundry, Hayle, c. 1890.

Harvey's crane traction engine, c. 1890, on the road leading to the Causeway.

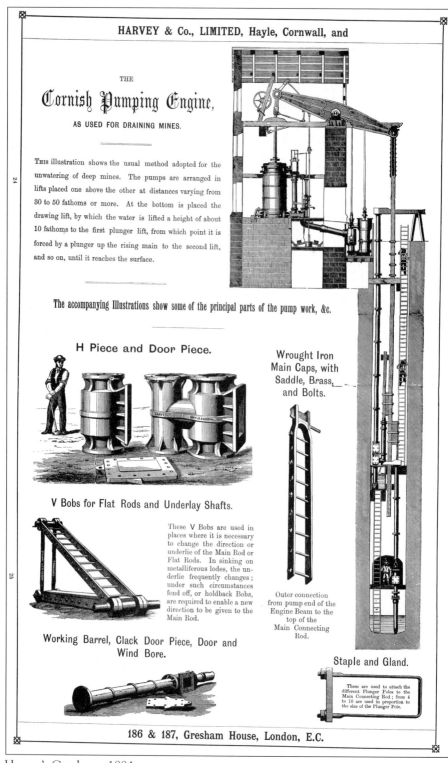

THE

Cornish Pumping Engine,

AS USED FOR DRAINING MINES.

THIS illustration shows the usual method adopted for the unwatering of deep mines. The pumps are arranged in lifts placed one above the other at distances varying from 30 to 50 fathoms or more. At the bottom is placed the drawing lift, by which the water is lifted a height of about 10 fathoms to the first plunger lift, from which point it is forced by a plunger up the rising main to the second lift, and so on, until it reaches the surface.

The accompanying Illustrations show some of the principal parts of the pump work, &c.

H Piece and Door Piece.

Wrought Iron Main Caps, with Saddle, Brass, and Bolts.

V Bobs for Flat Rods and Underlay Shafts.

These V Bobs are used in places where it is necessary to change the direction or underlie of the Main Rod or Flat Rods. In sinking on metalliferous lodes, the underlie frequently changes; under such circumstances fend off, or holdback Bobs, are required to enable a new direction to be given to the Main Rod.

Outer connection from pump end of the Engine Beam to the top of the Main Connecting Rod.

Working Barrel, Clack Door Piece, Door and Wind Bore.

Staple and Gland.

These are used to attach the different Plunger Poles to the Main Connecting Rod; from 4 to 10 are used in proportion to the size of the Plunger Pole.

186 & 187, Gresham House, London, E.C.

Harvey's Catalogue 1884.

Harvey's foundry 1890. Secondhand beams and miscellaneous castings can be seen on the waste ground below the Plantation.

A bob for a seventy inch cylinder diameter beam engine, in the yard of Harvey's foundry c. 1890.

Husband's Patent Oscillating Cylinder Ore Stamper at Harvey's foundry in about 1890.

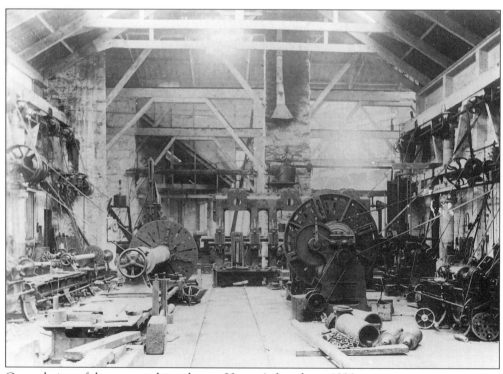

General view of the new machine shop at Harvey's foundry c. 1890.

Harvey's catalogue 1884.

Automatic four tank jigger built by
Harvey's c. 1890.

Three ton and 12 cwt steam hammers at Harvey's foundry in about 1890.

108

Fitting shop at Harvey's foundry c. 1890.

A recently discovered photograph of Cornish or Lancashire boilers and flues being test erected at Harvey's foundry c. 1870.

A crane engine pulling a compound-cylinder marine engine manufactured by Harvey's c. 1890.

SS Landore, c. 1891, was built by Harvey's. Her gross tonnage was 539 tons.

The launching of SS *Ramleh* in 1891. This was the largest vessel to be built in Hayle with a gross tonnage of 4,000 tons.

SS *Ramleh* leaving Hayle after fitting out in 1891.

Marine boilers constructed by Harvey's c. 1885. The boilers were 14ft 6in in diameter with a working pressure of 160 lb per square inch and are seen here in Harvey's boiler shop.

Ship repair was also undertaken by Harvey's. Here can be seen the steamer *Ethel* which had suffered damage to her bow.

Harvey's slipway and boat building yard c. 1880. Many a vessel was built on this slipway. Initially wooden sailing vessels were constructed, but from 1860 until shipbuilding ceased in 1893 ships were built using iron and steel.

HARVEY & Co., LIMITED, Hayle, Cornwall, and

MARINE ENGINES.

We have had large experience in the construction and manufacture of Compound Surface Condensing Engines for Marine purposes, and by using best material and workmanship can guarantee first-class results. We have Boats and Engines of our build at work in all parts of the world, particularly for Tug purposes.

These Engines with high pressure steam indicate from five to six times their nominal Horse Power, and are very economical with regard to fuel.

MARINE ENGINES FOR SCREW AND PADDLE BOATS, AND ON THE HIGH PRESSURE AND COMPOUND SYSTEMS.

ESTIMATES GIVEN FOR

ESTIMATES, DESIGNS, AND ALL INFORMATION GIVEN ON APPLICATION.

(The above Engraving represents a Compound Surface Condensing Marine Engine of 30 Horse Power nominal.)

ESTABLISHED OVER 100 YEARS.

186 & 187, Gresham House, London, E.C.

48

Harvey's catalogue 1884.

113

Hosken Trevithick and Polkinghorne Limited were general suppliers to farmers and were based at Loggans Mill. Seen here is one of their wagons and tractors.

Loading an HTP lorry on the wharf at Hayle c. 1930.

Seven
Gwithian and Godrevy

The National Explosives Company works c. 1900. The Mining Journal announced in 1889 that 'a manufactury for dynamite is to be erected on Hayle Towans in the parish of Gwithian... Messers Holman Brothers, Camborne, will erect the machinery, the surveyors are Messers Henderson and Sons, Truro, the local engineer is Mr George H. Eustace of Hayle and J.W. Wilkinson of Kennal Vale Gunpowder Works has accepted the management.'

National Explosives Works c. 1900. The form of the dunes was changed considerably. Small enclosures were made to avoid dangerous chain reactions if one of the small manufacturing plants blew up. On one notable occasion when an explosion did occur in a nitroglycerine plant, windows were broken in St Ives and the explosion was heard on Dartmoor. The new dunes, which were constructed to avoid the spread of such an occurrence, were planted with Marram Grass to keep the sand in place.

The National Explosives Works c. 1900. During the First World War the Hayle works supplied a large percentage of the cordite used in the shells for naval guns. At its height during the war over 1,800 people were employed on the Towans. The works finally closed in 1920 after the company went into voluntary liquidation in 1919.

Gwithian cliff and beach looking towards Hayle in 1950. The dunes behind the cliffs were once the site of the dynamite works shown in the previous three pictures.

Gwithian Church c. 1910. The overprinted 'A Merry Christmas To You' had been typed on before it was sent.

The old thatched chapel at Gwithian is hidden behind the village pub and is very rarely seen by passing visitors.

Gwithian is portrayed here by the photographer Robert Preston c. 1890. The lady seated behind the bank has an umbrella up; is it to protect herself from the sun or the blowing sand?

The buried church, Gwithian, c. 1880. It is more properly called St Gothan's Oratory.

Godrevy Lighthouse was built in 1858 following the wreck of *The Nile* on the 12th December 1854.

Godrevy Lighthouse 1890. This is the lighthouse that was immortalised in Virginia Woolf's novel *To the Lighthouse*, which she wrote while staying in St Ives.

Eight
Wreck and Rescue

Schooners, *Lizzie R. Wilce* of Falmouth and *Mary Browne* of Barrow were wrecked on Porthminster Beach on 7th and 8th of January 1908.

Three St Ives lifeboatmen outside the lifeboat station wearing cork buoyancy aids. This postcard was produced time and time again and it was not unusual for the name of a different town to be printed on the front although close examination shows it was in fact taken in St Ives.

Lifeboats have to be launched whatever the weather: this St Ives boat is making headway in a very heavy sea.

The St Ives lifeboat, *Caroline Parsons*, was wrecked on the Island when going to the aid of the *Alba*, 1st February 1938.

The *Alba*, a 3,700-ton Panamanian registered motor vessel from Hungary with its master Joseph Horvath from Barry, was bound for Civitaveccia in Italy with a cargo of coal when it went onto the rocks of Porthmeor Beach in 1938. The lifeboat, *Caroline Parsons*, capsized and was driven ashore after rescuing the *Alba*'s crew. All but five of the latter were saved, many by onlookers and coastguards who plunged chest deep into the mountainous seas. The coxswain, Thomas Cocking, received a silver medal and the crew, bronze medals for their service. The Hungarian government presented a Gold Cross of Merit to the coxswain and the Mayor of St Ives.

HMS Wave, seen here by the Ship A Shore Café, 2nd October 1952. A breeches buoy is in use. The vessel broke loose in the bay and drifted between Pednolver Point and the harbour.

The unfortunate *Othos Stathos* hit the rocks off Godrevy and was towed into St Ives on the 24th April 1913.

Flowergate was wrecked off Porthminster Beach, St Ives in 1946.

The Hayle lifeboat, Admiral Rodd with its crew on the 27th September 1907.

The Hayle lifeboat, *Admiral Rodd*, being launched at its inauguration on the 27th September 1907. The lifeboat service started in Hayle in 1866 and finally closed in 1920, this boat being the last one to operate from Hayle. A total of 95 lives were saved by this station.

Acknowledgements

I would like to thank the following people for the loan of photographs and postcards. Without their generosity this book would not have been possible:

Alan Curtis of the China Cat, St Ives; John MacWilliams, St Ives, and the Copperhouse Book Centre, Hayle.

In addition I would like to acknowledge the Cornwall Record Office for allowing me to peruse and have copies made of material deposited by Harvey's of Hayle (accession numbers, H DDH 215: 11, 12, 13, 19, 25, 29, 36, 40, 41, 52, 54, 62, 69, 71, and 89. H DDH 99, Husband's Patent).

I would also like to thank the Royal Cornwall Museum for some twenty photographs included in this collection and also Camera Craft, of Truro, for photographic printing.

A small number of photographs were also made available by the Penzance and District Museum and Art Gallery.